Sibling Shenanigans:

Brother-Sister Jokes

M. S. Gregory

ISBN: 978-1-922695-99-4
All rights reserved.
Cover designed by msgdragon

No part of this publication may be reproduced, distributed, or transmitted in any form or by any means, including photocopying, recording, or other electronic or mechanical methods, without the prior written permission of the author, except non-commercial uses permitted by copyright law.

Also by M. S. Gregory

- Cousin Chaos: Laughing with your Cousins
- Sibling Shenanigans: Laughing with my Sister
- Sibling Shenanigans: Brother-Sister Jokes
- Mum Seriously?! Teen-mum banter at its finest!
- What Cats really Think: Hilarious Cat Thoughts, Jokes, and Conversations That Will Make You Laugh
- From Bark to Snark: Sassy thoughts from your Pup

For permission requests, address the request to the author c/o
Permissions,
TAT Indie Publishing
triedandtrustedindie@gmail.com

1. Brother: "I'm really good at math!"
Sister: "Yeah? Then why do you owe me five bucks from last week?"

2. Sister: "I'm telling Mom you ate my candy."
Brother: "Go ahead... she already knows I ate it!"

3. Brother: "I'm teaching you a life lesson."
Sister: "About stealing my stuff?"
Brother: "No, about being patient while I take it."

4. Sister: "Stop copying me!"
Brother: "I'm not copying, I'm just making it twice as awesome."

5. Brother: "You'll never be as strong as me."
Sister: "Maybe not… but I can still hide your stuff."

6. Sister: "You never listen to me!"
Brother: "What? I never said that!"

7. Brother: "I'm older, so I'm in charge."
Sister: "I'm smarter, so I'm actually in charge."

8. Sister: "Why are you in my room?"
Brother: "I came to check if you're as annoying as usual. Confirmed."

9
Brother: "I'm going to eat all your snacks!"
Sister: "Good luck... I hid them where you'll never look."

10
Sister: "Do you know why I'm your favorite sibling?"
Brother: "Uh... no?"
Sister: "Exactly. You're not supposed to know."

11
Brother: "Why are you always in a bad mood?"
Sister: "Because you exist, obviously."

12
Sister: "Stop touching my stuff!"
Brother: "Relax, I'm just testing if you actually need it."

13. Brother: "Why are you always bossy?"
Sister: "Because someone has to keep you in line!"

14. Sister: "Stop stealing my clothes!"
Brother: "Relax, I'm just borrowing your style."

15. Brother: "I'm the favorite child!"
Sister: "Oh, please... even the dog knows I win."

16. Sister: "You never clean your room!"
Brother: "It's not messy... it's creatively organized chaos."

17. Brother: "I can eat faster than you."
Sister: "Sure... until I hide half the food."

18. Sister: "Why are you always annoying me?"
Brother: "I'm just keeping you entertained."

19. Brother: "I have superpowers!"
Sister: "Really? Which one?"
Brother: "Driving you crazy-instantaneously."

20. Sister: "Do you ever listen to me?"
Brother: "Yes... while I ignore half of it."

21) Brother: "I'm stronger than you!"
Sister: "Maybe, but I have better aim with water balloons."

22) Sister: "I'm the smarter sibling."
Brother: "Yeah... smart enough to annoy me constantly."

23) Brother: "I'm going to beat you at this game!"
Sister: "Sure... if cheating counts as winning."

24) Sister: "Why do you always get snacks first?"
Brother: "I'm faster... and better at sneaking."

25) Brother: "I can touch my toes faster than you."
Sister: "Cool... now touch your brain."

26) Sister: "Stop following me everywhere!"
Brother: "I'm just making sure you don't disappear."

27) Brother: "I'm older, so I'm smarter."
Sister: "Older maybe... smarter? Debatable."

28) Sister: "Do you even know how to clean?"
Brother: "Of course! I know how to move the mess around efficiently."

29. Brother: "I'm awesome at sports!"
Sister: "True... at hitting the wall with a ball."

30. Sister: "Why do you always copy me?"
Brother: "I call it 'strategic imitation.'"

31. Brother: "I'll beat you in a race!"
Sister: "Sure... after I give you a head start... of an hour."

32. Brother: "I know everything!"
Sister: "Except how to stay out of trouble, apparently."

33) Sister: "You think you're funny?"
Brother: "Yes... but I'll admit, you're funnier when you get mad."

34) Brother: "I'll hide your favorite toy!"
Sister: "Good luck... I already hid yours last week."

35) Sister: "Stop yelling at me!"
Brother: "I'm not yelling, I'm raising my voice to your level."

36) Brother: "I'm the best at everything!"
Sister: "Everything except being humble, apparently."

37 Sister: "Why do you always take the last slice?"
Brother: "Because I practice sharing... myself first!"

38 Brother: "I can beat you at chess."
Sister: "Sure... as long as the pieces don't move themselves."

39 Sister: "Stop touching my phone!"
Brother: "Relax, I just wanted to call your bluff."

40 Brother: "I'm the funniest in the family!"
Sister: "Yes... if making yourself laugh counts."

41. Sister: "Why do you always peek at my diary?"
Brother: "I'm doing research... for my autobiography."

42. Brother: "I'm an expert at video games."
Sister: "Right... and expert at blaming lag."

43. Sister: "Why is your side of the room a mess?"
Brother: "I'm testing gravity... it works perfectly."

44. Brother: "I can eat ice cream faster than you."
Sister: "Until brain freeze makes you cry."

45) Brother: "I'll scare you!"
Sister: "Not scary... just predictable."

46) Sister: "Do you always have to be right?"
Brother: "Not always... sometimes I just act confident."

47) Brother: "I can jump higher than you."
Sister: "Sure... but I can duck faster."

48) Sister: "Stop stealing my headphones!"
Brother: "I'm just borrowing your superior taste in music."

49) Brother: "I'm never wrong."
Sister: "Ah yes... the classic sibling logic."

50) Sister: "Why are you laughing?"
Brother: "Because I just thought about how mad you'll get later."

51) Brother: "I know all your secrets."
Sister: "Cool... then tell me how to stay calm about it."

52) Sister: "Stop copying my homework!"
Brother: "I call it 'collaborative learning.'"

53) Brother: "I'm the best at sports."
Sister: "Yep... at missing every goal."

54) Sister: "Why are you so lazy?"
Brother: "I'm not lazy... I'm energy efficient."

55) Brother: "I can scare you anytime!"
Sister: "Sure... but I can out-prank you all day."

56) Sister: "Do you ever clean the dishes?"
Brother: "I prefer to leave them as abstract art."

57) Brother: "I know how to fix things."
Sister: "Including your excuses?"

58) Sister: "Stop touching my makeup!"
Brother: "I'm just experimenting with chemistry."

59) Brother: "I'll beat you in hide-and-seek."
Sister: "Good luck... I already found your hiding spot last time."

60) Sister: "Why do you always annoy me?"
Brother: "I call it quality sibling time."

61) Brother: "I'm smarter than you."
Sister: "Smart enough to avoid your tricks, maybe."

62) Sister: "Stop hogging the TV!"
Brother: "I'm helping you practice patience."

63) Brother: "I can stay awake longer than you."
Sister: "Until your phone battery dies, right?"

64) Sister: "Do you ever help around the house?"
Brother: "Sure... I supervise very efficiently."

65) Brother: "I'm braver than you!"
Sister: "Brave enough to eat my cooking first?"
Brother: "Maybe not... okay, definitely not."

66) Sister: "Why are you always in my room?"
Brother: "I'm making sure you're not plotting against me."
Sister: "Or maybe I am..."
Brother: "Exactly my point!"

67) Brother: "I'm way stronger than you."
Sister: "Sure, but can you lift the remote when I hide it on the top shelf?"

68) Sister: "I'm smarter than you."
Brother: "Maybe... but I'm better at annoying you without getting caught."

69. Brother: "I'm the funniest in the house."
Sister: "Really? Because I laugh way more when you trip over your own feet."

70. Sister: "Stop taking my snacks!"
Brother: "I'm not taking them, I'm conducting a taste test... for science."

71. Brother: "I can beat you at any game."
Sister: "Any game?"
Brother: "Yes."
Sister: "Good... then lose gracefully."

72. Sister: "Why are you copying me?"
Brother: "I'm not copying, I'm creating a sequel. Your life: The Remix."

73) Brother: "I'm never scared."
Sister: "Really? Then why did you scream when the cat jumped on you?"

74) Brother: "I'm way cooler than you."
Sister: "Cooler? Sure... but I'm the one who knows all your embarrassing secrets."

75) Sister: "Stop messing with my stuff!"
Brother: "I'm just checking if you actually need it. Turns out... you do."

76) Brother: "I know everything!"
Sister: "Everything? Then tell me why your homework is never done."

77. Brother: "I'm braver than you."
Sister: "Oh yeah? Then try eating your vegetables first."

78. Brother: "I'm the fastest!"
Sister: "Fastest to do what? Run away from chores?"

79. Brother: "I'll beat you at hide-and-seek."
Sister: "Good luck... I already know where you hide all your tricks."

80. Sister: "You never clean your room."
Brother: "Of course I do... I just consider the mess a personal art installation."

81. Brother: "I'm the best sibling!"
Sister: "Best? Only in your imagination... and sometimes in annoying me."

82. Sister: "Why did you take my charger?"
Brother: "I wasn't taking it... I was temporarily borrowing it."
Sister: "Borrowing? You've had it for three days!"
Brother: "Exactly, temporary."

83. Brother: "I can beat you at video games any day."
Sister: "Sure... in your dreams. In real life, I'm still undefeated."

84. Sister: "Stop messing with my stuff!"
Brother: "I'm just testing if you actually need it. Spoiler: you do."

85. Brother: "I'm faster than you."
Sister: "Only when running away from chores, not responsibility."

86. Sister: "Why are you always in my room?"
Brother: "I'm making sure you're not secretly plotting against me."
Sister: "Or maybe I am..."
Brother: "Exactly my point!"

87. Brother: "I know everything!"
Sister: "Everything? Then tell me why you can't find your own socks."

88. Sister: "Stop copying me!"
Brother: "I'm not copying... I'm remixing your style. It's called sibling innovation."

89) Brother: "I'm never scared of anything."
Sister: "Then why did you scream when the dog barked?"

90) Sister: "Why are you so lazy?"
Brother: "I'm not lazy... I'm conserving energy for emergencies."

91) Brother: "I'm smarter than you."
Sister: "Smart enough to avoid your pranks? Maybe."

92) Sister: "Do you always annoy me?"
Brother: "Only on days that end with 'y.'"

93
Brother: "I'm the funniest in the house."
Sister: "Funny? You mean embarrassing yourself while I laugh at you."

94
Sister: "Why do you always take my snacks?"
Brother: "I'm testing my survival skills... turns out, chocolate is essential."

95
Brother: "I'm the fastest in the family."
Sister: "Fastest at running from chores, maybe."

96
Sister: "Stop yelling at me!"
Brother: "I'm not yelling, I'm broadcasting important sibling wisdom."

97) Brother: "I can beat you in hide-and-seek."
Sister: "Sure... if hiding under your own bed counts as creative strategy."

98) Sister: "You never do your chores!"
Brother: "I prefer to think of it as selective participation."

99) Brother: "I'm the best sibling ever!"
Sister: "Best? Only in your imagination... and maybe in annoying me daily."

www.ingramcontent.com/pod-product-compliance
Lightning Source LLC
Chambersburg PA
CBHW052046070526
44584CB00018B/2633